T0065608

DARE
TO SAY
"I'M HAPPY"

DARE TO SAY "I'M HAPPY"

PURNIMA L. TOOLSIDASS

PARTRIDGE

Copyright © 2016 by Purnima L. Toolsidass.

ISBN: Hardcover   978-1-4828-8714-3
              Softcover   978-1-4828-8713-6
              eBook   978-1-4828-8712-9

All rights reserved. No part of this book may be used or reproduced by any means, graphic, electronic, or mechanical, including photocopying, recording, taping or by any information storage retrieval system without the written permission of the author except in the case of brief quotations embodied in critical articles and reviews.

Because of the dynamic nature of the Internet, any web addresses or links contained in this book may have changed since publication and may no longer be valid. The views expressed in this work are solely those of the author and do not necessarily reflect the views of the publisher, and publisher hereby disclaims any responsibility for them.

Print information available on the last page.

To order additional copies of this book, contact
Partridge India
000 800 10062 62
orders.india@partridgepublishing.com

www.partridgepublishing.com/india

Index

Preface

This book was not really meant to become a book! It happened quite by accident, due to my meeting a number of young women, all well-to-do, educated and sophisticated. I was struck by the similarity in their sulky expression, and the way they responded to my greeting.

'Hello! How are you?' I asked.

'Oh, fine! How are you?'

Then, without waiting for my reply, they launched into a detailed listing of all their woes.

Had the woes been serious, they would have had all my sympathy; but when people have so much that they get dissatisfied, there is something not quite right!

It would be funny if it wasn't so sad. I found almost an identical attitude in the successful young men. These people – any age between thirty and fifty – have nothing left to struggle for. They have no major problems, except their own dissatisfaction with themselves.

I found that this phenomenon was common to the affluent educated everywhere. It seemed likely that many would go into acute depression unless they pulled themselves up.

By the grace of my Guru, Swami Akhandanand Saraswati, I have learnt some worthwhile lessons. The best way I can express my gratitude is to pass on some of these lessons and hope that they will help others, as I was helped.

Hence, this book.

Purnima L. Toolsidass

November 2007.

Chapter I

Dare to Say

Why do we hesitate to speak about our happiness?

I'm not talking about youthful comments like, 'I feel great today'. The youth is, thankfully, uninhibited and expressive. That is, unless an unhappy childhood causes an overwhelming shyness that psychologists describe as emotional insecurity. What the hell – all of us are emotionally insecure in some way or another; and that is why we hesitate to proclaim our happiness! And, in restraining ourselves from stating that we are happy, we begin to wonder whether we are happy at all. This doubt sows the seeds of emotional beggarliness.

Our society is currently facing an epidemic of the virus that I call EP. EP stands for 'Emotional Poverty'. The symptoms are too subtle to be caught until they are too strong to be cured. Not that it is impossible to cure this disease; there are doctors and there is a treatment for it, but it is not easy to find a competent doctor, and the treatment often costs more than the patient is willing to pay.

Anyone who wants to be happy, and is not afraid to pay the price, will benefit by analyzing his own impulses and reactions in day to day life.

How easily do you get angry? Anger is a sign of helplessness. It reveals lack of self control as well as lack of control over the situation. It gives a false sense of relief that is temporary. It gives a false sense of power when the recipient shows fear or submission. It gives an illusion of being 'in command'.

Why do you tend to stuff yourself, eat too often, see movies that are filled with violence and sex, want more and more sex, more and more money, more and more drink, more and more of a good time? 'It's natural!' you'll say. 'Who doesn't?'

I counter that with a question: Are those who give way to all natural impulses, really happy?

That brings us to the question of what 'happiness' is. There are charming booklets that say 'Love is...' and 'Happiness is...' but the emotions they speak of are so fleeting that it misleads us into thinking that we have to keep chasing them, if we want to be happy. It deludes us into a false complacency as soon as we feel happy, and then creates a void as soon as it is gone.

Well, what is happiness? Someone said, 'Happiness is not a destination; it is the journey.' I believe that it is the destination as well as the journey. However, to go on a journey we must know where we want to go, and why we want to go there, and which the best way to travel is. We must also know what we will need on the way.

We have come to a stage where we have almost stopped thinking for ourselves. Our mind is too busy planning our day, the tasks in hand, our social position, our position at work, the movies we want to see, the next holiday we must plan, and the revenge we must take on whoever said or did something we didn't like. We add to our mental hassles by watching movies that demand our attention and add excitement to our already overexcited mind. Then we indulge in sex, drinks and gluttony to obtain temporary relief. Gradually, our system demands higher and higher doses of escapist relief and a new cause of tension is built up. An increased irritability and a hidden fear that higher doses will become ineffective some day eat into us, driving that elusive factor called happiness further away.

J.K.Rowling gives us a hint in 'Harry Potter and the Deathly Hallows', when Dumbledore tells Harry that he left the clue for Harry in a children's book because people like Lord Voldemort never take children's stories seriously. What an amazing insight! If we take this tip and enjoy little things, instead of brooding upon all that is annoying, how much happier we could be – and, it's free!!

I have seen this in myself and in others, that some kind of an unspoken superstition stops us from admitting – even to ourselves – that we are happy. Maybe it is the old tradition of the evil eye, or of gods being jealous. It may be that we like to indulge in self-pity and martyrdom! It is heroic to bear heavy burdens and show people how much we have to endure. We get social acclaim for our nobility and sacrifice, whereas we get only envy if we admit we are happy.

This is a paradox, because modern lifestyle teaches us to always show that we are 'on top' of our problems. To admit that we can't cope is considered a sign of weakness. So, we always paste a bright smile on our public face and refuse to admit that we're human, with human needs and weaknesses. At the same time, we misbehave and excuse ourselves on the grounds of having 'pressures' and needing that outburst or indulgence!

Aren't we a bit mixed up? Do we know that we are mixed up? Do we think about how to untangle ourselves? Do we want to be happy or are we happy to remain tangled?

If the reader is happy being tangled, I suggest you close this book straightaway. If you are eager to be truly happy, I suggest you read on for a while and see whether it helps you to find the courage to say, 'I'm happy!'

Chapter II

Say I'm Happy

Say 'I'm happy' and you will feel happier.

As soon as you say, 'I'm happy', there will be a clamor of voices in your head telling you about all the problems you have.

Take some time off, and jot down your problems. Then, consider them one by one. Divide them into groups, like practical problems, emotional problems, spiritual problems, health problems, financial problems, etc. Grade their seriousness. Examine in a detached manner and check the extent to which each problem affects you, and whether you can find a way to reduce the problem or not.

It is quite extraordinary how we build up imaginary problems, like imagining that the assistant at a store looks down at me, or that my colleague looks down at me because I'm fat.

We get upset because we fail to get the desired response from people we interact with. Examine why you get upset with X. Is it because he is unreasonable or because your expectation is unreasonable? How does the other person perceive your behavior, your expectation, and your feelings for him? Our relationships are created gradually. Very often the initial goodwill leads to expecting more and more understanding and help. We have our moods, our good and bad days, and expect X to understand; but when the same happens to X, we feel hurt! Then we express our hurt by becoming aloof, and X feels doubly hurt by our behavior. Goodwill gives way to grievances. It becomes a problem and we don't know how to handle it. Pride won't allow us to say sorry. Self respect prevents us from admitting that we were unfair. Ego asserts itself and makes us pretend we don't care. Saying, 'I'm happy' won't work, because it's not true.

Nobody is perfect; pointing out faults continuously only makes matters worse. Accepting our fault each time doesn't always help either, because people like to shove the blame on someone else and tend to have an insufferably superior attitude! So, what's the answer?

The answer lies in analyzing, discriminating and balancing. Honesty is the first requirement. Generosity is the second, and humility is the third. We also need to consider the nature of X and gauge his responses and future behavior when we admit our mistake, blame him for his, or try to discuss the matter objectively. No two people are alike and there are no readymade formulas for interpersonal problems.

All problems in life can be condensed into two basic types:

1. Not getting what we want.
2. Getting what we don't want.

Some of these problems can be removed by effort. Some can be removed by simply giving up wanting. Most have to be 'lived with', and knowing how to 'live with' them is half the battle. A great many problems are automatically removed if we are generous enough to accept the fact that if X does not respond as we want, he is entitled to his reasons for doing so. Little things like daughters not dressing the way we want, or sons not eating proper meals become major causes of friction without achieving anything.

Lack of appreciation and loneliness are the most common causes of depression and dissatisfaction in life. The first can be reduced by questioning your motive for what you do. Are you cooking a meal/putting in additional effort to get appreciation, to be popular, to get a promotion or to clinch a deal? Is your effort motivated by a sense of duty or is it done simply because you want to give X some pleasure and comfort?

If we don't understand the feelings that prompt our actions, we unconsciously expect several returns and side benefits. You cook lovingly, and it will give you peace if you expect nothing more than to see your loved ones enjoy the food. It is the desire for appreciation that leads to disappointment when they don't express the appreciation you crave. If it is clear in your mind that your goal was their pleasure, just watching them eat with relish will satisfy you, because you will know that your purpose has been achieved. If they tell you how lovely the food was, it will be a bonus. If they don't say anything, it will not make you unhappy even if you feel a bit disappointed. All too often we make the situation worse by remaining silent, when things would be made happy all around if you'd just asked, 'Did you like it, love?' If something went wrong and the food wasn't what they like, you can't blame them for not raving over it or falling over backwards to tell you how much they appreciate the hard work you'd put into it anyway! Would you have had the maturity to do that when your mother cooked for you? Faced with their criticism, if you can just express your feelings, 'Darling, I'm so sorry it didn't turn out right,' will bring you the reaction, 'It doesn't matter love, I know you tried!' and the situation will change to one of friendliness and understanding. You can say proudly, 'I'm happy!' even if the meal has been a disaster!

All too often we exaggerate things beyond proportion. We suffer and so do others. This habit starts from the pleasurable feeling of negative excitement, and the comfort of self-pity it brings. When we lack real satisfaction, we try to obtain it from diversions that give excitement or pleasure. This is a trap that is common and very easy to fall into. Well, having trapped ourselves, we have to wrench ourselves out of it; and no doubt there is a wrench when we pull away. But then, nothing comes cheap, especially not freedom!

Being under someone else's control is not pleasant, but none of us can claim to be completely independent. If we are financially independent or we are emotionally dependent; and if we are happy in emotional dependency, we can be sure that it won't endure! The emotional dependency doesn't have to be for a person. It can be for food, drink, drugs, lifestyle, or anything else. Our lifestyle gears us to expect happiness from different sources as we grow up, and as we grow older. We chase one goal after another, and even if the goal is obtained, it is too transient to satisfy us for long.

The sages say that the moment that comes between the fulfillment of one desire and the rising of the next desire, is happiness. Put in another way, lack of desire is happiness. Put in another way, complete mental, physical, emotional and spiritual comfort is happiness. Anything that disturbs this condition is a cause of unhappiness. But, it is not possible for us to hold on to this condition, so what do we do? Go on being happy and unhappy by turns?

No. We are not playthings for others to twist and turn. We are not zoo animals that have little choice but to eat what is given and make the most of their prison cell. We are humans with options and intelligence. So, if we make ourselves the puppets of those who can reduce us to laughter or tears by a word, look or deed, we are being very foolish, and throwing away our right to be happy. That is much worse than not having freedom of speech or the right to vote.

'This is a free country!' Yes, but how free are we? There is no happiness without freedom. There may be comfort, but not joyfulness. Living in a free country is not worth much if we remain slaves to preconceived notions, to inhibitions, to our moods and our cravings. We just have to look at the wealthy people in the free countries to see how few of them are truly happy or at peace. So many sell their souls for wealth, glamour, popularity or power, and find it was a bad bargain!

So, what is a good bargain? A good bargain is when we give something gladly and are glad to just get the satisfaction of giving it. Even though people don't think this out in such clear terms, this is why so many people derive immense satisfaction from animal welfare work. When we do something for an animal, we have the scope to give love for the joy of giving. There are no complications like getting praise or a return favor. There is no fear of future misunderstandings or quarrels. An animal never lets us down, because we expect nothing from it.

It's not easy to start, but once we get started, it is like a great weight lifted from our shoulders, if we do everything with the same attitude as doing animal welfare work. After all, we are all animals, too, even though we lack their innocence and charm! Mother Teresa lifted diseased, dirty beggars off the streets of Calcutta. Thousands of nuns joined her. They lived in crowded rooms, ate simple meals, had few comforts or conveniences, and no entertainment except the deep satisfaction of doing something worthwhile without expecting anything. That was their greatest luxury and it is a luxury that is beyond any earthly luxury. No wonder they radiated happiness wherever they went. Would they have exchanged this joyfulness for the luxury of being the Queen of England?

'Well, I'm not Mother Teresa,' you'll say. Quite so! There was only one Mother Teresa. But, she gave us a glimpse into the Kingdom of happiness, and we need not be Roman Catholic to take the tip!

We'll talk about this in the next chapter.

Chapter III

Taking a Tip

In the last chapter we spoke about Zoo animals having no option but to suffer. We are, by the grace of God, born human, and born free. We have the capacity to think and plan and choose. Yet, so often we see people who shut them up in self-created cages of rigid ideas and expectations. Desires enslave us. They whip us into submission, making us do all sorts of things we know to be wrong. We hurt others and hurt ourselves. We need an Abraham Lincoln to set us free. The tyranny of the mind is much worse than any other tyranny, and this is the truth that is hinted at in every epic and every mythological story, fairy tale, and folk lore. We read out 'Red Riding Hood' to our children; do we ever think about who the wolf is?

Freedom – or independence – is the primary requisite for happiness. We have to be free of fear, free of desire, free of prejudice, free of partiality, free of superstition, free of emotional dependence. Not possible? Who says so? Possible is a relative word, and total freedom is not necessarily attached to it. Say, like Napoleon, 'Nothing is impossible', and you will find yourself capable of much more than you'd thought possible!

We will be happy to the degree to which we can free ourselves from the expectations that create unhappiness for us. Every step forward is a step towards greater happiness.

We spend far too much time in brooding about the past, planning for the future, wondering about what other people think and do, and resenting things that are utterly unimportant. We forget that there are just 24 hours in a day. Time management is just as important as managing our finances, children, business and hobbies. More, in fact, because none of the others can be well-managed unless time is utilized well. How we rush through every task, to be able to watch that show on TV or have a game of golf! We want to have this game or watch that show because it is fun, and what is life without fun?

And, what is fun? Why do we desire to have fun? How does it benefit us?

What a stupid question! Everybody wants fun, because life is such a pain if there is no fun in it!

Why does life become a pain? Why can't we enjoy life like a child?

I think the story of Adam and Even and the Garden of Eden perhaps, signifies why life becomes a pain, a drag; dull, full of friction, fear and daily chores. Maybe the forbidden fruit symbolizes the first impulse of a desire for something more than what is rightfully ours; the greed for more, even when our basic needs are fulfilled.

I cannot believe that desire is wrong; it is only when it is for something wrong that desire becomes wrong. Just as anger serves a useful purpose when it is used against injustice and exploitation, desire for the right things is needed for human progress and happiness. Desire becomes harmful only when it becomes excessive or obsessive, or for the wrong things. Or, when it encroaches on the rights of another. Then, it destroys the power to discriminate between what, or how much, is right and proper. Once discrimination is lost, we lose the ability to respect the rights of others. And, unhappiness sets in, because we can never be happy if we cause suffering to any other.

Mother Teresa knew that the way to be happy was to spread happiness, which also means reducing the suffering of others. She knew that that could be done successfully only if it was done as a complete gift, without any expectation of any return. Every person has this knowledge, hidden deep in the heart. The knowledge gets smothered under extraneous considerations, and happiness eludes us.

What I am writing applies to every human being, regardless of age, sex, country, creed, or social status. It applies to the healthy and to the physically challenged. It applies to the wealthy and the impoverished. It applies to the religious and the non-religious. Don't we see beggars laughing and chatting? Don't we see orphans enjoying themselves and don't we see a glow of goodwill on the face of cancer patients or a crippled old woman? Why is it that some people are unhappy even when they have so much, and some people are happy even when they have so little?

The theory of Advaita Vedanta believes in the non-duality of the Brahman who is the substratum on which the whole of creation is built. It says that when that Brahman pervades the interactive world, it is called the Paramatma – the totality of all the Atmas (souls) that are attached to individual bodies. Be that as it may; it can neither be proved, nor disproved. The interesting thing is that modern science is also telling us that at the bottom of all creation is a pure energy, and that the solid objects are actually particles that are floating in a kind of fluid essence. DNA also tells us that while we are individuals with genetic qualities that have come down from generation to generation, we are all composed of the same basic matter as the rest of creation. Carl Gustav Jung was a Swiss Psychologist and a contemporary of the famous Sigmund Freud. His theories were ignored until fairly recently, and I suspect that they were taken seriously only when the psychologists realized that Freud's observations left much to be desired. Jung has spoken of 'the collective unconscious'. His findings are based on personal experiences and insights. They are impressive and undeniable. They confirm that there is a factor that connects all beings, and that every human has a subconscious that craves for higher ideals. He calls it 'the collective unconscious.'

One doesn't have to be a psychologist to understand that a person cannot be happy unless his basic needs are fulfilled. Freud wrote much on the evils of repression, but he did not elaborate on the evils of over-indulgence. He failed to understand that in avoiding repression, people would be unrestricted in their efforts to satisfy their appetites, and that this would become another – even more dangerous – disease in the long run. This is the disease that is, in my opinion, symbolized by the forbidden apple.

Chapter IV

The Forbidden Fruit

As I said earlier, desire is harmful either when it is for something that is wrong, or when it is disproportionate and uncontrolled.

The mind is like a child. Children are very quick to take advantage of the slightest hint of weakness in adults. They get spoilt by over-indulgence, and they become juvenile delinquents when the love and discipline in their lives are not properly balanced. It is the same with the mind.

The mind is a part of the body, and like the body, it needs food, water, air and rest. Food is the work we do (including thinking), water is the love we get and give, air is the relaxation, and rest is the satisfied feeling of having done something that enhances our self-respect. How can we be happy if the mind is not healthy? If the mind is healthy, we can be happy even if the body is unhealthy, but the reverse is not possible. An unhealthy mind is not a sick mind; it is a mind that is deprived of one or more of its basic four needs. If these basic needs are met, the person can be happy even if he is alone, unappreciated, poor, or physically challenged.

However, nobody can be happy if they fill their minds with desire, anger and greed. The Bhagwad Gita says that these are the three paths to Hell, and John Bunyan says much the same thing in 'The Pilgrim's Progress.' All the evils in our life stem from these, and any or all of these can successfully steal the happiness from our lives and hearts. They can not be killed. Too strict a control will result in a back-lash. The only solution is to divert their flow.

Desire can be channeled towards everything that is noble and praiseworthy. Anger can be channeled into opposing all that is harmful to us and to others. Greed can be channeled into acquiring good qualities and doing good deeds. Actually, desire is the mother of anger and greed. When desire is thwarted, it makes us angry. When desire is fulfilled, it makes us greedy for more. So, diverting these is the only solution and no psychologist can disagree.

No religion can disagree with this, either. I am sure that God would be very happy if all religions focused on the ideals common in all religions, instead of quarreling over the minor differences of implementation! What is God, if not another name for goodness, and what is goodness unless goodwill for all is in the heart? And unless there is general benevolence for all beings, how can anyone be at peace, or experience enduring happiness?

So the Garden of Eden would symbolize a Heaven that is filled with goodwill, and man has to leave it when deceit and ill-will are allowed to sully a pure place (the heart, or the inner world). If this story can be used to stop us from being harsh, demanding, unreasonable and selfish, it will have achieved something eminently desirable. It can help us create a little Garden of Eden of our own.

All this is very nice to hear, but what can we do when we are dealing with nasty, selfish, unreasonable people? How can we be happy when the boss is arrogant, unpleasant and unreasonable, or the wife is jealous, suspicious and full of avarice? How can we continue to be nice when the children disrupt our lives, throw tantrums and indulge in every bad habit and activity? How can we be pleasant to unreasonable neighbors who are a continuous nuisance and unbearably boorish?

Again, there is no quick-fix answer to life, and we just have to remember that we cannot have a perfect world. Modern science and affluence have brainwashed us into thinking that we can solve all our problems with money power and muscle power. 'Buy him off, or shoot him', is the way criminals think. Little children either cry, or hit out. Cultured adults try to make their homes sound-proof and have a drink to blank out everything unpleasant from their minds. They certainly don't live in the Garden of Eden! They have eaten the forbidden fruit for sure.

No, the intelligent person is prudent, and handles it differently. He will, first of all, not allow the situation to become so bad that it can't be improved. He will control his desires and impulses, so that a little sensible give-and-take makes life more harmonious. Having fewer expectations will mean less interpersonal friction, less disappointment and less frustration. It will also mean wasting less time on unprofitable activity and acrimonious interaction. Instead of rushing from one hassle to another, and leading an exhausting life of unabated excitement, he will ensure that his mind gets the rest that is so vital for mental health and the happiness we all seek. Instead of drowning his negative feelings in drink, drugs, sex or violence, he will allow his mind to recuperate by providing it with the four basic needs of food, water, air and rest.

All of us react more than we act. We react to others and others react to us, and then we react back! Only when we are at peace with ourselves can we create an atmosphere of peace, and control our reactions. Try this in any city in the world. Get onto a crowded bus and wait for someone to bump into you. You can either say, pleasantly, 'hold on, be careful,' because the person has either lost his balance or his manners. Or you can say, 'Are you blind? Can't you see where you're going?' in an angry voice. The reaction of the other person is perfectly predictable. A pleasant remark will bring a pleasant response and an angry response will bring an angry retort, almost every time.

Why only people? Even animals respond in like when people show anger or affection! They can't control their responses, but we can. And by controlling our responses, we can control the responses of people we deal with. Each person has a personality, and that personality brings him cooperation or problems. Personality is something quite different from beauty, age, wealth, skill, etc. As someone said, 'Charm is something that cannot be defined. If you have it you don't need anything else. If you don't have it, it doesn't matter much what else you have!'

My personal understanding of charm is a genuine benevolence seen in the smiling eyes of a person I may or may not know; may see in person or on the screen; may talk to or listen to, or simply observe. We are 'charmed' because our soul craves love, and we feel attracted to whoever has genuine love to give. Not a cheap physical infatuation that people mistake for the real thing, but a deep unmotivated goodwill that wants nothing except universal peace and happiness. That is real love. That is the love of God and the saints and that is what is increasingly missing in our lives. This is as acute a need as physical hunger, and this is why people crave sex at any price – it is the closest substitute for the love their soul yearns for.

Now, to get love, we have to give love; and love is as difficult to define as happiness, because they are inseparable. The closest example to real love was considered to be a mother's love for her baby, a dog's love for his master, or a monk's love for God. These days, people laugh if these examples are given and say, 'Don't be naive!' They say that a dog loves his master because his basic needs are provided by the master, but if that was so, the zoo animals would love their keepers with the same devotion. People used to accuse Mother Teresa of helping lepers because she wanted to please Christ! People say that mothers don't really love the baby; they love themselves and see the baby as a part of themselves. We can argue about these matters till doomsday, but argument becomes a waste of time unless it serves a purpose.

Deriding love will not help to enhance it. Let us take it that all love is selfish. I love my baby, my dog loves me, and a nun loves God, and we all do so for our own selfish reasons. Well, if selfish love makes us better people, happier people, people who make the world a better place, is it not better than not loving, or loving with the intention to control and manipulate?

It is quite true that all love is selfish. Even the highest love is based on the heart's desire for fulfillment. To a monk or nun, it is the heart's earnest desire to obtain God. For a dog, his master is his god and he wants to please his master. To a mother, her baby is her joy and life, and seeing her baby happy and growing well, is what makes her happy. Well, when we aspire to a goal that is considerably loftier than self-gratification, we evolve as human beings. We are able to touch the elusive happiness, and experience as pure a form of love as possible.

Love is an urge to give comfort and happiness to another; it is not the urge to get pleasure from that person or object. No doubt we get pleasure, too, but that is a side benefit. It is not the motive. All kinds of problems and complications start when we miss this basic truth. We feel happy when we are not disappointed or frustrated. Having no expectations saves us from disappointment and frustration. This is why love and happiness go hand in hand.

But when we try to grab something without having love, it becomes the forbidden fruit. When we want to impose, dominate and possess, we leave the Garden of Eden and create Hell, because love is essentially the art of giving, not of taking.

Chapter V

The Art of Giving

Happiness depends on learning this art. A person has no control over his or her birth. We cannot choose our parents, place of birth, appearance, or abilities; we can only try to improve upon them. I don't want to bore the reader with the various theories of karma that result in the circumstances we are born into. Nor do I want to dismiss it as God's will. We cannot deny that some people are born with advantages and some are not. However, we are all born with the capacity to make choices. We can learn how to give, and if we learn the art of giving we will learn the art of being happy.

True giving is when we give simply because we feel good to give. All the religions emphasize on giving alms and doing charity. The importance of charity cannot be denied, but it has the handicap of almost always leading to vanity. The donor feels proud to have 'given', and this pride is so heady that it pushes out everything else from the mind, and the person feels that none of his lapses matter, since he's such a wonderful fellow! Charity thus becomes counter-productive.

Even if the ego doesn't swell to that extent, the very purpose of selfless giving is lost when we get praise and public acclaim for what we have done. Charity becomes a business transaction when it is used to build up the public image of a person. It becomes just one more way of attaining celebrity status or adulation.

Charity – or giving from the heart – need not be restricted to money or material items. In fact, it is people who have nothing but money to give, who give money and try to appease their conscience for their selfishness and meanness. Real giving comes when we care, when we have genuine good-will, when we wish to bring some comfort, solace or pleasure into someone's life, and our only motivation is the urge to spread harmony and happiness.

It is charity when we return a soft answer to a rude comment; when we understand that the person is rude because he is troubled or sad. It is charity when we smile and say 'thank you' to someone who is just doing his duty when he opens the door or serves the coffee you ordered. It is charity when you help an old lady carry her parcels up the steps, or hold the baby while a mother settles her bags on the overhead rack of a bus. And, this charity is another name for love. It is true generosity of heart. It is sensitivity and grace, and it brings a light into the eyes of the giver and the receiver. It links two souls and helps to make the world a happier place.

It is up to each of us to decide whether we want to trigger off a chain reaction of pleasantness or unpleasantness. The latter is easier and gives us an illusion of strength. The former takes a bit of resolve initially, but is far more rewarding in the long run. This reminds me of a little verse about a smile, that I'd read when I was a child.

'A smile is quite a funny thing; it wrinkles up your face. And when it's gone you'll never find its secret hiding place. But far more wonderful is to see what a smile can do; you smile at one, he smiles at you, and so one smile makes two!'

Unfortunately, I cannot remember who wrote it; but I tried it and it worked!

Unfortunately, it worked for frowns, too....

I found myself frowning when someone frowned at me, until I decided that that was not the chain I wanted to be a part of. So, I smiled extra brightly when someone frowned at me, and the astonished expression on his face was priceless! It was such fun to see the person look utterly taken aback and confused that I wanted to repeat the experience. I felt the day was brighter for having broken the chain; both for me and for the other guy.

Then I thought I'd experiment by smiling at people who looked gloomy, sad or sullen. To see a sad face lighten and see brooding eyes brighten, is to see a ray of sunshine on a gloomy winter day. 'Happiness is like jam – you can't spread even a little without getting some on yourself', they say. The same holds true for grumpiness, and we get what we give. So, why not choose to give and get smiles and goodwill?

Even if we come across the odd exception, it's still worth it, because we develop the ability to laugh off frowns!

Its funny how being happy makes us better able to deal with unpleasantness, disappointments and harassment. I have observed that the same things can, on some days, be brushed aside effortlessly; but on other days they seem insurmountable problems. I have also observed that bad luck seems to dog me on the days I am irritable or tense; that people are more cooperative and helpful on the days I'm happy. This is not a mere coincidence. Anyone can observe the same phenomenon in their lives. I believe that this is because of the aura created by our frame of mind. This subtle aura is understood by the in-built radar we all have. It warns a prudent person when not to speak! Fools ignore it; thick-skinned people are unaware of it; but every sensitive human being can avail of it if they are alert and smart.

This same built-in radar can help us select who needs a kindly word or a gentle smile, and how we can best help others in little ways even when we can't do great things.

When I was at school, my English teacher once gave us a thought-provoking topic for an essay. The subject was, 'The importance of trifles'. I started the essay by saying that trifles were unimportant – they were trifling matters. But as I wrote on, the thoughts developed on their own, and at the end of the essay I realized that I had written that in the long run, it was the little things that mattered most in our lives. And, to this day I do believe that giving of ourselves in little ways creates a happy little inner world for both me and the other; and that I have been at the receiving end much more than at the giving end, in the 68 years of my existence!

I find that the more I give, the richer I feel. And, it's not money I'm talking about. You know that, don't you?

Chapter VI

Wealth

We spoke of feeling rich in the last chapter, and this reminded me of a very profound definition of poverty made by my Guru. 'Poverty is the feeling of lacking something,' he'd said.

How often has that little sentence helped to pull me up! How rich I have felt because of it, whenever I overcame any desire for anything! It has enhanced my self-respect when I was in the midst of people who were fabulously rich, beautiful, intelligent and famous – all because I could see that thanks to God and my Guru, I was free of many of their cravings, jealousies and emotional insecurities!

I have seen peace on the faces of monks and nuns. I have seen peace on the faces of beggar women who were merely skin and bones and surrounded by skinny, naked children. I have seen it on the face of a bitch suckling her puppies on the pavement. But, I rarely see it on the faces of the wealthy, successful, fashionable, and young.

It is a paradox that the very people who have so much, seem to be so discontented; while those who have so little seem to be at peace. It would be foolish to imagine that all poor people are at peace, or all who are blessed with good fortune are unhappy. But it would help us be happy if we understood the reason for their having peace (or lack of it) in their own circumstances.

There is a little story about the 'Trap of ninety-nine'. The story is that a King was once looking over the ramparts of his castle. He saw a small mud hut that was built along the castle wall. A poor potter lived in the hut with his wife and two children. He made a few coins by making and selling pots every day. The wife would buy whatever provisions she could, depending on the previous day's income, and the family would share the food. The King saw them laugh as they ate together, and shared their experiences with each other.

The King was surprised that this poor family could live together so happily, because with all his wealth and power, his life was always filled with unending problems. 'What is the secret of their happiness?' he asked his Minister.

'Your Highness, it is because they have not fallen into the trap of ninety-nine,' answered the wise old man.

'What is the trap of ninety-nine?' asked the King. 'Can you explain it?'

The Minster told the King that he should continue to observe the potter's family. He threw down a bundle with ninety nine rupees in it. The next morning, the potter woke up and saw the bundle. He called out to his wife, who came running. They opened the bundle and were astonished to see that it contained ninety nine rupees. They wondered where it could have come from.

'Keep it carefully,' said the potter. Now that we have ninety nine rupees, let us try to save one rupee so that we have a capital of a hundred rupees.' The wife agreed.

The King watched the family and saw that now they skimped and saved. There was constant friction and dissatisfaction. The children cried because they were given less food. The potter grew bad tempered because he tried to get higher prices for his pots. The potter's wife grumbled because the potter couldn't increase his daily production.

Gone was the peace and content they once had. For what? For one rupee; for a rupee that would turn their wealth of ninety nine rupees into a hundred rupees. They were happy when they had no savings; but they became unhappy as soon as they got ninety nine rupees!

Would you agree that they were richer when they had no savings?

There is another similar story that left a strong imprint on my mind. It is about a businessman who expected to make a profit of a billion rupees. His calculations went wrong, and his profit turned out to be only ten million rupees. He went running to his Guru. 'Maharaj! I am ruined!' he said. 'What happened?' asked the Guru. 'I should have made a profit of a billion, but I miscalculated badly. I am ruined!' he replied. 'Did you lose all your wealth?' asked the Guru. 'No, Maharaj, but instead of making a billion, I made only ten million!' wept the man. Do you feel pity for the poor man, or do you feel like laughing?

There is yet another story of a wealthy businessman who came to my Guru looking very sad. Guruji had heard that he had done well in business, so he asked what the matter was. 'I heard you have done well,' said Guruji. 'Am I misinformed?' 'No, Maharaj, I have made a very good profit this year.' 'Then what is wrong? Why do you look so dejected?' asked Guruji. 'Well, you see, it is because my competitor's profit is much bigger than mine!' explained the businessman.

That's proportion of wealth for you! Like Einstein's theory of relativity, wealth and happiness are relative, and not necessarily connected. We allow a lack of money, and the things money can buy, to make us believe we are poor. We feel poor even when we have so much. Why? Because we haven't learnt how to segregate material wealth from inner wealth. And, until we learn to do this, we will never be really happy.

To be rich means to not be poor. It means having all we want and not wanting or expecting anything from anyone else.

We make ourselves poor when we depend on others to respond as per our expectation, or do something we want them to do. It is an inner poverty to allow our happiness or satisfaction to depend on another person's behavior. We are that much the happier if we make up our mind to remain unaffected by praise or criticism, or by the absence of little gestures that mean so much, or by some unwarranted rudeness.

This is not impossible. Even if we can't achieve it fully, we'll be that much the richer for reducing our dependency. Much of what we perceive to be rudeness is unintentional. We make ourselves unhappy when we expect another to live up to our standards, which are often beyond their ability or understanding of what we expect.

We make ourselves unhappy when we see another having more than we have – this is reversed as soon as we see another who has much less than what we have. So – it's up to us to decide which one we choose to look at. We can see the glass as half empty, or as half full! It's our choice whether to make ourselves dissatisfied because we have 'less', or thankful because we have 'more'. Again, less and more are relative, as long as our basic needs are met.

If you dare to say, 'I'm rich', you are rich indeed.

Chapter VII

Six Enemies

The Indian philosophy exposes the six enemies of happiness, accepted by modern psychology. These are desire, anger, greed, attachment, vanity and jealousy. These are natural to every being and necessary for our survival and progress, so we are not to destroy them, we are merely to canalize them in a way that they help to push us ahead instead of pulling us back.

We have got into a rut of presumption. We presume that we will be happy if we get the things we desire. We think that we'll be happy if we are married to the man we love; we'll be happy if we get the job we want; we'll be happy if we get the car we like, etc. There is no end to the things we desire; starting from any material object, or change in appearance, or the approval of someone who matters to us. It is quite true that all of these will bring a temporary state of happiness, but it is equally true that this happiness will soon pass because other desires will arise as soon as these are fulfilled. As long as unfulfilled desires fill the heart, we can never really be happy.

Anger is the reaction of our wishes being thwarted. Its intensity depends on the intensity of our desire. The more we want a girl, the angrier we'll be if someone else wins her. It may just be that we didn't get the dish we wanted for supper, or that there were no tickets for the show we particularly wanted to see. And, the result of anger is our hurting the one we love the most, resulting in our getting angry with ourselves, over and above the anger we feel for the other! And, who can ever be happy if anger blocks the flow of happiness in the heart?

While the thwarting of desire leads to anger, the fulfillment of desire leads to greed. These three are considered to be the gateways to hell, because they continue in a vicious and never ending cycle, linked to each other and bolstering each other. It is obvious that a greedy person can never be happy because it is one of the characteristics of greed to be unending.

Attachment is the dormant cause of desire, anger and greed. We desire only that, to which we are attached, and we get attached to a person, object, place or situation because it gives us pleasure. Attachment blocks happiness because it is inevitable that we have to, at some stage in life, part with whatever we are attached to. Either that person or object will leave us, or we will be forced to leave them.

In our search for happiness it is natural to strive for personal development and success – that generally goes hand in hand with wealth and fame and satisfaction. Vanity is the direct result of these achievements, and it becomes our Achilles heel, because it is impossible that we will always be clever, rich and successful. Even if we are, the fact that there are others who are clever, richer and more successful will hurt our ego and make us unhappy.

Jealousy is called the green-eyed monster, and is indeed a dangerous enemy to happiness. Even if we have everything we desire, and everything we need, we can never be happy if we are eaten up by jealousy.

Jealousy is a byproduct of possessiveness, dissatisfaction with what we have, and with what we are. People who are content and self confident are less likely to be troubled by the demon of jealousy.

So, if we want to be happy we must use our IQ and our EQ to turn these enemies into friends.

The way to turn jealousy into a friend is to ask ourselves why we need to be jealous. If another person has qualities we lack, we can develop the qualities we have, so that we need not feel inferior. When the qualities of the other person are God given qualities like a high IQ, good looks, and wealth, we need to understand that happiness does not depend on these qualities.

If we are jealous of the other's popularity, we have to examine whether the popularity comes from his ability to entertain lavishly, or his ability to help others. The popularity that comes from lavish entertainment is meaningless. The popularity of helpfulness can be achieved by anyone who is willing to extend help. It may be an unpalatable truth, but if you do not like helping people, you have no right to resent the popularity of someone who does help people. If you want to stick to your self-centered life, stop reading this book and give up all hope of enduring happiness.

To get rid of the vanity that is a major block to happiness, look at others who are higher placed than yourself, in whichever field you are vain about – including social work. No matter how rich, beautiful, intelligent, or successful you are, there will be someone who has achieved more. Seeing him will cut you down to size, and then you will stop treading on air and making enemies, because of nobody likes an egoistic man or woman.

It is said that all the slaps we get in this world hurt, not us, but our vanity! It is our ego that is angered when someone is rude or refuses to do what we want. It is our ego that is hurt when another woman is better dressed, or another man gets the contract. Vanity leads to jealousy and both are disastrous for happiness. One way of making vanity a friend is to be vain about not allowing vanity to rule you!

Attachment is needed to make life meaningful. It must be based on an impersonal affection, acknowledging the fact that the person, place, object or situation to which you are attached is a gift, but it is not permanent – because nothing is permanent – and that you will not resent its going when the time comes. After all, don't we enjoy each season, without getting terribly upset that summer doesn't last the year round? Don't we enjoy Christmas, knowing it has come for just a week or so? Khalil Gibran has written, in 'The Prophet', 'Your children are not your children. They are the sons and daughters of Life's longing for itself. They come through you, but not from you. And, though they are with you, yet they belong not to you.' So, enjoy the objects of your affection without wanting them to be permanent.

Come to think of it, what is it that we can call 'ours' in every sense of the word? There is nothing over which we have full and lifelong control – not even our mind, body, or life. So, by just facing this truth we can turn attachment into a friend and enjoy it while it lasts and let it go painlessly when it is time for a change.

Greed is perhaps, the easiest to convert into an ally. We just have to become greedy for the important things in life. They are the things that give bring deep happiness. And, nothing gives greater happiness than giving happiness.

There is a little story about a saintly man called Dada Vaswani. He lived in Pune, India. At that time, Pune was just a small town near Mumbai. Dada Vaswani was going for his morning walk when he saw a small group of children giggling as they picked up the shoes of some construction laborers who were working at a nearby site. He asked them what they were doing. 'Oh, we're just having some fun,' they said. 'We'll hide the shoes and when the men come, we'll have fun watching them search for their shoes.'

'Shall I show you a way to have real fun?' asked Dada Vaswani?' The children were all too ready for fun and agreed instantly. Dada Vaswani took some coins from his pocket. 'Put one rupee in each shoe. Then hide, and watch their faces when they come for their shoes at the end of the day's work,' he said. You can imagine how good the children felt to see the joy shining on the faces of the poor laborers, when they found a rupee in each shoe – a rupee meant a lot in those days! The children learnt a valuable lesson that day; a lesson about real fun. A lesson that turned a mean outlook into one of kindness.

Anger can be constructive as well as destructive. If it is used against all that is wrong in this world, it will make you an ethical, proactive person, who works for the betterment of society. Such a person is always admired and respected, and getting these enhances our self image, bringing happiness into our lives and the lives of others.

There are lots of little ways for controlling ourselves from saying harsh things impulsively. 'Count 10' is a well known and popular method. Another method is a self imposed penalty – like missing out on something we like for a week! A third method is to imagine we are in the presence of someone we love and respect. These little tricks gradually become a habit and save us from uttering hasty, hurtful words that result in so much bitterness and regret.

Desire makes us unhappy because it is endless, so the way to use it is to want to be happy with what we have. Contentment is the antidote and a very pleasurable antidote. It can easily be attained by realizing that the glass may be half empty, but it is also half full! It is like the quote, 'I had no shoes and complained until I saw a man who had no feet.' No matter how little we have, there are those who have even less. No matter how legitimate our desires are, they are our enemies if they block our ability to be happy.

It is not possible to avoid the desire for a child to get well, or our husband to get a good job, but it is possible to say, 'Well, at least it is not worse. We still have much to be thankful for. Times will improve. Good days will come. I refuse to allow sorrow to erode my existence.'

Chapter VIII

Poverty

One of the wisest men I've known was my Guru. He has defined poverty as 'the feeling of lacking something.'

Give it a bit of thought, and you will gasp at the implications!

By this manner of measuring, a power hungry Emperor can be a beggar and a contented beggar can be termed an Emperor!

Let us give a thought to how many kinds of needs we have. One is the basic need for food, shelter and clothing.

The second is money to spend for comforts and luxuries, for pleasure and entertainment.

The third is money for achieving a status symbol, doing charity that brings acclaim, or allows you to play with power politics.

Of these, only the first is a basic essential; the second is important, but the extent is relative. The third is an ego based need that is insatiable and leads to other needs. And, 'need' is a form of poverty, so even the wealthiest man or woman can be poor in terms of not having 'enough'.

Then, there is the moral poverty that gives an excuse to people to cheat, steal, kill and indulge in other illegal and immoral activities. People justify this by blaming their circumstances, saying they had an unhappy childhood, or that they were traumatized by some mishap, or something they saw. I do not say that their reasons are invalid, but I would certainly say that they are crippling themselves by not being open to the fact that others have overcome worse situations and they can also develop the will power to overcome their problems if they want.

Emotional poverty is, perhaps, the most pathetic. Most of us have seen how an emotionally dependent person becomes a slave, or a toy in the hands of unscrupulous people. Emotional poverty is not limited to wanting another to show love, or affirm them. It is emotional poverty when a bully needs to show his strength and power by beating up a weaker person. Such bullies are by no means confined to back alleys – they are found in schools, and every walk of life. They flourish in Corporate Houses, and in the corridors of power, and in welfare groups and even in religious groups! In fact, there is nowhere they are not present; eyes gleaming with meanness, malice and spite, relishing the satiation of their little megalomaniac tendencies! Little do they realize that they are actually exposing their inner poverty, their lack of self-respect and self-confidence. People who are self assured and satisfied have no need to stutter or prove themselves to be 'in control'!

Signs of most of these can be seen in a growing child, and the time to ring alarm bells is when you see signs of cruelty to an animal or a younger child. Fortunately, people realize the need to check traits of violence or incontrollable temper as early as possible, but success cannot be assured unless and until the adult person wants to get rid of his inner poverty.

To be able to say, 'I'm happy' we need to be emotionally rich.

We all know how hard we have to work to get material wealth. We all know that material wealth is not enough for happiness. We all want to be happy, and we must be prepared to put in the requisite effort. We are willing to work for our supper, we are willing to work for a favor. Are we willing to work for our happiness?

It's a strange paradox that a man will spend a thousand dollars to get a diamond bracelet for the woman he wants to bed, but he will think ten times before giving a hundred dollars to help a child with cancer. I wonder what people would choose, if they gave the matter some thought and compared the degree of happiness they get from a night out, with the happiness of giving a meal to orphans in a home.

Paradoxically, we can never be happy if we only think about how we can increase our own enjoyments. It is a paradox that we can be happy only when we think about how we can spread happiness (or reduce the suffering) in this world.

When we think about how we can be happy, our focus is on what we lack, whereas when we think about how we can make others happy, our focus is on what we have. The first makes us feel poor; the second makes us feel rich. It doesn't need much calculation to know that we feel happy when we feel rich; nor does it take any calculation to understand that we feel rich when we are loved, and that we get love when we give happiness and love to others.

People who want everything for 'me and mine' are poor indeed! How can such pitiable specimens ever hope to be happy?

People who want everything for 'me' and 'mine' suffer because they consider themselves to be their body. This illusion is so common and so strong that they never even think about how foolish it is to identify with something that we can live without, and over which we have limited control. For example, you say, 'my hand', but you never think that you can't be an object you possess. You will continue to live even if your hand gets cut off or is affected by paralysis. If someone hurts your hand, you unconsciously accuse him of hurting you. This is not merely a figure of speech – it is an indication of how strongly you identify with something that is not really you.

In the same way, we all say, 'my friend, my husband, my boss, my child, my dog' etc. We allow an emotional relationship to possess us to such an extent that we feel that they rule our lives. This emotional dependency is a self inflicted bondage. It is abject poverty.

To be happy we have to learn to love them without being emotionally dependent on them, because a person has to be free to be happy.

Our emotional dependency affects others as adversely as it affects us, so when we gain the ability to love without binding, it not only sets us free, it sets the people we love free, too. The same applies to those we hate or fear. Bondage is a burden for all, so when we free ourselves, we free others and the result is an improved relationship all round. Being free makes us happy; seeing our loved ones happy makes us happy, so happiness is multiplied when we can love without attaching strings to our love or getting upset when others do not come up to our expectations. Then, even a person with no money will not feel deprived in any way!

Chapter IX

Fear

Fear never leaves us. We feel fear when we are rich and we feel fear when we are poor. We feel afraid of sickness, of losing a loved one, of losing out on something, of being left behind or being left out. Fear results in a thousand adverse reactions and consequences. It can be a justified fear or it can be irrational. Fear is always a hindrance to happiness.

Fear is not something anyone can escape from – it has to be faced. Taking pills, drugs, or therapy is not the answer. Not is it of any use to bluff ourselves by saying that we don't care. We must analyze what we fear and why we fear the things we are afraid of.

Basically we fear that, which can disrupt our comfort – like sickness – or that, which we do not know – like death. All our fears come within these two categories, whether it is the fear of growing old, financial difficulties, losing face in society, or a loved one leaving us.

If we make a list of all the things we fear, we will find ourselves laughing at our own immaturity. Old age, for instance, is something most people fear, even though they know it is inevitable. The same holds good for death and loved ones leaving us. Then, we fear unexpected misfortune.

We have to make two columns – one column has the inevitable events for which we can prepare ourselves and the other column has the events we can neither foresee nor prevent.

The first column has to be dealt with by preparing ourselves emotionally and practically. 'Yes, I will grow old, but I will develop my interests so that I enjoy new hobbies instead of getting lonely and depressed. I will manage my finances so that I need not depend on anyone else for my day to day expenses.' It is amazing how much relief you can get by planning to face the inevitable with a positive attitude. Of course, it will work only if you accept the fact that much as you enjoy your present life, it is by no means the only way to enjoy life.

The second column also has to be dealt with by preparing yourself emotionally. 'Yes, I may die in an accident. I may get cancer. Anything can happen to the one I love any day. There is nothing I can do to foresee the future or change it. What I can do is to enjoy what I have today. I can be grateful for each day that passes in peace and comfort. I can live today in such a way that I leave behind happy memories for others when I die; and I will be rich with happy memories if anything happens to my loved one.'

It is easier for those who have faith in God. Only those who lack faith tend to blame God when faced with sorrow or disaster. 'Why did God let this happen to me?' Why should you think that you are the favored one to whom nothing bad should ever happen?

The law of Karma gives the only logical explanation for the misfortunes and inequities we see all around, but it is, after all, a matter of belief. Some people don't want to accept that their suffering may be caused by their past wrong deeds. They prefer to lash out at an unseen, unknown factor and blame 'God' for being unjust, irrational and whimsical. We see this behavior in little children, when they howl and kick and fight against the punishment given by a responsible parent to cure them of some undesirable trait. The kids are innocent enough to get over it the next day and come and hug their mother and say, 'Mummy, I love you.' Adults miss out. They hug their resentment and take it out on others because they have no faith, and they don't want to accept that their suffering could have any rationale. This is fear, hidden so deep inside that it is not even known for what it is.

A person who feels fear becomes a cripple unless he teaches himself to deal with it and get on top of it. To dare to say, 'I'm happy', you have to pull up your socks and get on top of the known and unknown fears that loom up when least expected.

To get on top of fear, you have to know that you are not merely a body. Nor are you a body with a mind. You have a soul that is indestructible. You are that soul.

'Ha! Ha!' say the cynics. 'How do you know? If you have a soul, show it to me. Prove that I have a soul! I have no time for religious hocus pocus!'

Well, my friend, I cannot accept your challenge to prove that I have a soul and so do you and so does everyone else. I can only give a counter challenge, asking you to prove that none of us has a soul! You can't.

So, since neither of us can establish that what we believe in is correct, let us consider which belief brings us a greater advantage. This is like playing a game – imagining either one or the other premise; but the stakes are high. What is at stake is the ability to say, 'I'm happy.' It is the ability to not only say, 'I'm happy', but to be happy.

Chapter X

Faith

We have faith in little things, but our faith even in what we believe, is so fragile that it is unable to support us when we need it the most.

Faith can neither be defined nor explained satisfactorily. It cannot be bought, or won, or earned. It is a gift that some people have naturally, and it is a source of tremendous power that can be utilized to remain unshaken in a crisis or to give succor to someone who is in dire straits. It can, however, be developed by a sincere effort.

Faith in God is the most common and also the most uncommon! People who have faith go to a place of worship, or pray at home. They go to pilgrimages and they wear some jewel or cross that acts as a reminder and gives reassurance. The test of faith comes when things go wrong. To believe that there is something good in whatever happens, is the greatest faith and it enabled the early Christians to face hungry lions in a Roman circus, or people face the gas chambers of Nazi concentration camps. Such faith does not come easily – we have to face a trial by fire to know whether we have it or not.

Faith can be cultivated by reading about people who had immense faith, but we have to be vigilant that faith does not turn into a blind faith that leads to misuse of philosophies or adulation of the wrong kind of people. Unscrupulous crooks, impersonating messiahs and pseudo Gurus are all too common. People who crave for some form of emotional support fall prey to their wiles.

People often say, 'I have faith in myself.' If questioned, they are hard put to explain exactly what they mean. Usually, it boils down to a faith in 'managing' things, and nothing more! They say faith, but what they actually mean, is self confidence. Sometimes, it is just another word for arrogance or over-confidence! And that is not faith – it is folly!

Having faith in another person is good up to a point, but every human being is fallible. So, while on the one hand faith can be a source of great strength it can also be a cause for utter disaster! We have to analyze the kind of faith that helps and the keep away from blind faith that misguides us and leads us into wrongdoing.

If a person can cultivate faith in a benevolent higher power that can neither be proved nor disproved, it can keep him away from any number of bad habits, immoral activities and social evils. That, in itself, is a benefit that cannot be achieved by any other method.

The practice of confession and being given the last rites has the power to make a person feel absolved of all his sins. The same feeling is aroused when a Hindu bathes in the holy Ganga. Psychiatrists charge high fees to convince their patients that they should not have a guilt complex. The results of both methods are similar, but the first is inexpensive and works at a deeper level of the subconscious mind. So, even if it is all a sham, is it worth discarding or laughing at?

The feeling, 'God loves me', is priceless! If you say, 'There is no God, so how can he love me?' who do you harm, but yourself?

A child believes that his mother loves him. He grows up and gets married and his wife convinces him that his mother's love was possessive and mercenary; it was not love. Only she loves him truly. The man becomes bitter and stops meeting his mother. The old woman is left hurt, lonely and unhappy. The younger woman rejoices in her triumph as long as she is enamored by her spouse. Then they have their differences and part ways. Has not the man and his mother lost something very precious because the wife wanted to prove that the man's mother didn't love him?

'Fools rush in where angels fear to tread,' is a common phrase. A lot of sadness is created when people are too eager to expose the 'truth', and leave no scope for compassion or understanding. Justice is blind, they say, and they forget there are very few clear cut truths and only a thin line separates what is right and what is wrong. Faith in a higher power moderates the cruelty of blurting out the bare truth, unless it is necessary and helpful for people. Faith gives compassion, and compassion is always in short supply!

Faith gives us the strength to say, 'I'm happy.' But, it has to be the right kind of faith.

The faith we really need is to believe that our happiness does not really depend on any of the things we feel we can't do without. We have to believe that no matter what happens, the indomitable spirit within has the capacity to be at peace. We have to realize our own potential for emotional independence, contentment and serenity. This faith can come from religion, but it can come regardless of religion. In fact, religious scriptures are often confusing and contradictory. The people who interpret them for us may be disruptive forces that destroy even the faith we have in simple values. That is why I love the statement in the Bhagwad Gita, when Krishna tells Arjuna to 'give up all religion and come to me.' The 'me' refers to the spirit – or innate knowledge of good and bad – in all. Faith in this innate knowledge helps us to be happy and help others be happy. It can save us from dogma that often destroys the basics of godly principles.

Death is inevitable. Everything that is born has to die. As Shakespeare said, 'A man can die but once, and every man owes God a death.' True, but you can also say, 'A man can live but once, and we owe ourselves a life well lived.' And then, have the faith that you will live well; you will live happily.

That is the faith worth having!

Chapter XI

Obstacles

What are the obstacles in our getting the right kind of faith? Unless we recognize them, how can we overcome them?

The first obstacle is the identification with the body. The second is the identification with the mind. The third is to believe that happiness comes with material things and other people.

We are brainwashed by the opinions of other people and consumer oriented media blitzing. We need to sit back and think whether people who have all that we think is necessary for happiness, are happy. We need to think about why people who have none of these things are happy.

Then, we have to ask ourselves whether it is happiness we want, or whether it is the things or people? An honest answer is essential. Otherwise the entire exercise is futile.

If you want material objects or people, give up your wish to be happy. If you want happiness, accept the fact that you may need to make some tough choices.

The choices are not really as tough as you'd expect. We don't have to give up anything, really. What we have to give up is our dependence on things like food, comfort, reactions of others, and expectations for things like a rise in the pay packet, or getting expensive things at a discount!

Most of us know the feeling of frustration when we can't afford the things we'd like to have. The obstacle in our happiness is not our not having the things – it is our allowing our desire for them to spoil our pleasure in the things we do have. So, if we want to be happy, all we have to do is decide that our happiness depends on what we have; it does not depend on anything else.

Many of us read of tragedies and meet people who seem to have given up hope due to some personal loss. Every group has some cynics who revel in grumbling about the world going to the dogs, and declaring that it is no use trying to do anything. How can they ever hope to be happy? They need to meet some of the proactive people who just never give up trying to help! One such lady is Mrs. Sudha Kaul. I was charmed by her when I went to the Institute For Cerebral Palsy in Kolkata, India. One of the patients she pointed out was a young man in his early thirties, sunning himself on the terrace on a winter morning. 'This is Karan,' she said. Later I learnt that Karan was her son. When he was a little boy she learnt that he had cerebral palsy and she also learnt that Calcutta (as it was called in those days) had no institute for such children.

Sudha did not break down and give up. She contacted people, educated herself in how to deal with children with special needs, and started an institution with her garage as the office. The Institution is now a landmark. God knows how many children it has helped, and how many parents have been spared of the trauma Sudha must have faced. She never speaks of it, but the compassion and goodness she radiates is, in itself, a therapy for troubled people.

Thinking of Sudha makes me think of others like her. Mahatma Gandhi's non-violent resistance to British rule was triggered off because of the way he was insulted for not being a white. Anne Frank's diary has become an inspiring book because she faced the Nazi holocaust. Mother Teresa won the respect of the world because she decided to do something for the destitute people and lepers in Kolkata. Helen Keller turned her personal misfortune into a gift for countless millions. The list is endless. Each of these people found happiness because they chose to not sit in idleness and wallow in cynicism.

As long as we have a body and mind, we will have physical and emotional needs. These needs become an obstacle to our happiness if we let them; but they can also generate immense happiness if used intelligently. The trick is in using our intelligence constructively and knowing that happiness is not beyond our reach.

Learn to tell yourself, 'I want to be happy, I can be happy even when things go wrong. I will not let circumstances stop me from holding on to my inner peace. The disturbances are temporary – why should I let them spoil my day? My body may age or rot, my spirit is eternally youthful. Hope is my birthright – nobody can steal it from me unless I let them.'

I do not say that this is infallible, but I do believe that it is effective in creating happiness and – more important – preserving it!

Chapter XII

Happiness

Indian philosophy has analyzed that there are five faults, or causes, that prevent us from reaching and retaining happiness. They are called 'kle`sha'.

The five kle`shas are:

1. Avidyaa (ignorance)
2. Asmitaa (pride or vanity)
3. Raaga (attachment)
4. Dve`sha (aversion)

5. Abhinive`sha (thinking that we are the body)

If we understand these five, we can overcome them, and attain enduring happiness. Faults are vulnerable. They start leaving us as soon as they are recognized. If we don't give them shelter, they are unable to stay with us.

Ignorance means the ignorance about our real, eternal Self, our Soul, the Atma that is never born and never dies. It means ignorance about the transient nature of the world and about how we believe ourselves to be controlled by external factors. 'Vidyaa' means knowledge or skill; 'a+vidyaa' means lack of vidyaa. When we gain the knowledge about the metaphysical reality and know that we have an inner strength that enables us to overcome every sorrow, the misfortunes and the things we crave no longer have the power to agitate us. We know that the gift of happiness is within us and we have the power to hold on to it.

'Pride comes before a fall', is a common proverb which most of us agree with, but ignore! The sages say that most of the blows we receive are blows to our ego, our pride, our vanity. Even a doorman has the power to upset us if he shows the slightest lack of attentiveness! How often have we lost our temper just because it hurt our pride when someone ignored us, or was rude or impatient! How often have we quarreled with loved ones – not because of what they said – but because of the way it was said? We live on the precipice of pride and even the most insignificant person has the power to push us over the brink by hurting our pride! It is pride that makes us unhappy when someone else is more talented or successful. Can you imagine how happy you would be, if none of these things had the slightest effect on you?

Attachment is not only for people or possessions; it is also for ideas, places, habits, etc. The slightest disruption in any of these – even when the toast is not exactly as brown as we like it – can make us gloomy and irritated! We are enslaved by our attachments and they lead us to a merry dance, holding our happiness hostage at every point.

It is the same with aversion. Attachment and aversion are two sides of a coin. They always go together, and it is a toss out as to which is stronger. To live without someone or something to which we are attached is often easier than living with a person or place we hate. Be that as it may, there is no doubt that these have to be banished if we want to retain our happiness.

The greatest block to remaining happy is the fear of death, because death is inevitable and it is unknown. It takes courage to face what we fear, but it is easier to face what we know than to face the unknown, and this fear is connected to the body, because it is the body that dies, not the soul.

It is not easy to stop identifying with our body, because our body is the instrument by which we live. We are affected by hunger and pain, sleep and fatigue, and restlessness or feeling energetic. There is a powerful mind-body connection that is common to humans and animals. Every living being experiences hunger, fatigue, fear and lust. Animals do not have the capacity to analyze them or control them, but humans do. Unless we utilize this capacity, we are no better than animals – worse in fact! That is why we need laws to protect the weak from the strong, who can misuse their power to abuse and exploit the weaker. Animals have their own codes of conduct even when they live in the wild. Most of us have seen deer graze peacefully near a lion. They know that the lion has eaten and they are safe until he feels hungry again.

Not so with humans. Humans are the only people who indulge in violence just for kicks, or out of uncontrolled anger. All these are a result of the five basic faults mentioned above. The more a person is able to control and overcome them, the closer he is to happiness.

Swami Vivekananda said that every man is potentially divine and it is the responsibility of each of us to develop the divinity in us. My interpretation of this is that we all have the potential to understand and overcome the causes that drag us down; the causes that make us unhappy, and cause us to behave in a way that brings unhappiness to others.

What is 'divine'? We use the word divine to express appreciation for a food item, a dress, an experience, or beautiful scenery.

Another way of expressing divine is, 'out of this world', and that really means something that is uncommonly desirable. So, wouldn't enduring happiness be divine, too? Wouldn't a state of mind that is serene and content, unruffled by the storms of the world be divine?

The question is – can an ordinary human being reach such a state? This needs to be analyzed further. What is 'ordinary'? What is 'human being'? And, what is the state we want to reach?

I am convinced that ordinary refers to anyone who is willing to exist, rather than to live. I feel that an ordinary person is one who is too lazy or too foolish to try to be happy by using the methods given by the sages, have proved to be effective, and are psychologically sound. A human who is willing to live as helplessly as an animal is ordinary. He cannot hope to obtain more than some fleeting pleasures that he takes to be happiness. In this category I include the millionaires who are seeking new thrills constantly, and the politicians who seek more power merely to satiate their urge to control.

What is a human being? To my mind, a human being is a person who displays humane values in every situation. A human being is a person who is aware that life has a higher existence and a lower existence. He is not satisfied with the lower existence, but strives for inner self-improvement that elevates a human to divinity. History has plenty of examples, but we lack the courage to follow them. If we are to merely eat, drink, procreate, sleep, and do our daily chores, can we truly claim to be better than animals?

And, what is the state we want to reach? It is a state of peace. Peace means contentment – not craving anything and not fearing anything. Can we reach that state?

Our mind is influenced too much by the opinions of other people. They are ordinary people, convinced that external factors like wealth, success, physical pleasure, etc are essential for happiness. We accept this because we have been brainwashed by what others say. We have not learnt to think for ourselves. We have not yet learnt that there is no reason for us to be ordinary people. We can never be happy until we learn that we have the ability to be happy even when we do not have the things that the world considers essential for happiness! We have to be able to depend upon what our heart tells us, what we know to be right and wrong (or true and false) for ourselves, and have faith that the power that rules the fate of the world is a positive power and an active one, and it helps all those who seek genuine happiness in the right way.

Can this be done by anyone?

Well, that depends on each individual! Men (when I say men, I mean a human being of either sex) have shown us that it can be attained. We may not be a Buddha, but there is no doubt that there is ample scope for each of us to rise, and continue to rise to a higher level of inner existence and a greater degree of enduring happiness.

The first step to this is to dare to say, 'I'm happy!' Believe that happiness is in you. Believe that your happiness is not dependent on anything except your attitude, your outlook. Get over the habit of seeking sympathy and help from others. Give up the pride that causes anguish when others think that you are vulnerable and lack something. Stop imagining that possessions or people will make you happy. Stop thinking about the illness or death that you may have to face. You have no control over the future. Whatever comes, you can face it better if you do not fear it. Besides, there is every likelihood of its not coming at all! So, why cripple yourself with unprofitable speculation?

As soon as you are convinced that you can be happy, that you are happy, happiness will spread a golden hue over all you think and do. The positive radiation of happiness spreads happiness to others in your vicinity, and happiness is multiplied, and the ripples keep returning to you, making you feel happier. This is not an illusion, it is not a myth, it is not magic, but it is magical in its authenticity and effectiveness.

Now, it's up to you to bring it into your life! It's up to you to dare to say, 'I'm happy!'